Preface

You don't know who it is.

Or you do know, but they don't.

Or you know who it is, but you think it might also be someone else.

You might feel it's going to happen, that, yes, you've read all the signs right – it's inevitable.

Or logic tells you it's never going to happen.

Ah yes. Love.

Don't worry. You're not alone in these soul-wrenching uncertainties. The human mind has always been a bit too caught up in them for its own good. And Irish people, being human, are no exceptions. As we see from what follows, lovers have been prepared to use any means necessary – singing, guessing, charming, arranging, cursing, versing, brewing or just talking – to get their way.

They usually didn't get their way. Nothing changes.

ANTHONY BLUETT

IRELAND
IN
LOVE

SELECTED BY

ANTHONY BLUETT

MERCIER PRESS

MERCIER PRESS
PO Box 5, 5 French Church Street, Cork
16 Hume Street, Dublin 2

A CIP is available for this book from the British Library

ISBN 1 85635 139 4

10   9   8   7   6   5   4   3   2   1

Printed in Ireland by Colour Books Ltd.

Contents

1

Charms, Potions, and Curses

Love, like agriculture, is ruled by uncertainty. It's no surprise to find that all sorts of more or less dubious techniques were used by those in love to ensure that they got what they wanted, and kept it once they had it.

A LOVE POTION*
LADY WILDE

Some of the country people have still a traditional remembrance of very powerful herbal remedies, and love potions are now frequently in use. They are generally prepared by an old woman; but must be administered by the person who wishes to inspire the tender passion. At the same time, to give a love potion is considered a very awful act as the result may be fatal or at least full of danger.

A fine, handsome young man, of the best character

---

* From *Quaint Irish Customs and Superstitions.*

and conduct, suddenly became wild and reckless, drunken and disorderly, from the effect, it was believed, of a love potion administered to him by a young girl who was passionately in love with him. When she saw the change she produced in him by her act, she became moody and nervous, as if a constant terror were over her, and no one ever saw her smile again. Finally, she became half deranged and after a few years of a strange, solitary life, she died of melancholy and despair. This was said to be 'The Love-potion Curse'.

To Cause Love*
LADY WILDE

Ten leaves of the hemlock dried and powdered and mixed in food or drink will make the person you like to love you in return. Also keep a sprig of mint in your hand till the herb grows moist and warm, then take hold of the hand of the woman you love, and she will follow you as long as the two hands close over the herb. No invocation is necessary; but silence must be kept between the two parties for ten minutes, to give the charm time to work with due success.

---

* From *Quaint Irish Customs and Superstitions*.

A WICKED SPELL*

LADY WILDE

When a girl wishes to gain the love of a man, and to make him marry her, the dreadful spell used is called *Drimial Agus Thorial.* At dead of night, she and an accomplice go to a churchyard, exhume a newly-buried corpse and take a strip of the skin from the head to the heel. This is wound round the girl as a belt with a solemn invocation to the Devil for his help.

After she has worn it for a day and a night she watches her opportunity and ties it round the sleeping man whose love she desires; during which process the name of God must not be mentioned.

When he awakes the man is bound by the spell and is forced to marry the cruel and evil harpy. It is said the children of such marriages bear a black mark round the wrist, and are known and shunned by the people, who call them, 'sons of the devil'.

* From *Quaint Irish Customs and Superstitions.*

INCANTATIONS[+]

PADRAIC O'FARRELL

A strong insurance could be brought about by offering one's betrothed a drink over which the following incantation was said:

> You for me and I for thee and no one else,
> Your face is mine and your head turned away from all others.

It has never been decided, as far as I am aware, which spells or charms had the greater power for there was one available to stir up dissension between a pair of lovers too. A handful of clay was taken from a new grave and thrown between them.

The following words accompanied the throwing:

> Hate ye one another! May ye be as hateful to each other as sin is to Christ or as bread eaten without blessing is to God.

A custom still surviving is that of unmarried maidens hopping around the Metal Man, an iron monster that points to the treacherous rocks in Tramore Bay. Hopping around three times ensures marriage within a year.

---

* From *Superstitions of the Irish Country People.*

That hopping reminds me that if an introduction to the 'Old Boy' himself, the Devil, is desired it can be brought about by hopping around the Black Church at Tulla, Co. Clare, saying one *Our Father* backwards.

LOVE'S CHARMS*
SÉAMAS Ó CATHÁIN

The practice of giving a draught or a drink to a young man in order to coax him or win his love was very much in vogue in Ireland long ago. The drink was usually given by the girl who intended to gain the boy's affection, though it appears that quite frequently the dose was administered by the girl's mother.

The effect of this drink was the development of an over-powering love and infatuation for the individual in question. This affection could last for months and would be abnormal while it lasted, but it seems that after a time, or after the couple had been united in marriage, a violent reaction often set in and the love was changed to bitter hate and loathing.

Marriages contracted while individuals were under the influence of this love potion generally turned out to be most unhappy right from the start. Such couples seemed to be destined to do nothing but quarrel during their wedded lives. It was also commonly said that after

---

* From *The Bedside Book of Irish Folklore*.

a young man partook of such a drink, there was a distinct possibility that he might go out of his mind, especially if the wind should change within twenty-four hours.

One of the many examples quoted of such derangement is that of a certain itinerant who spent his days travelling through the baronies of Erris and Tirawley in north Mayo. In his young days, it was believed, he had been a blacksmith and he went by the name of Gabha na gCraobh, his home place being the townland of Creevagh near Ballycastle on the north Mayo coast. He had very eccentric habits and his odd ways were popularly explained by the belief that he had been at the receiving end of a love potion followed by a change in the wind.

These love potions were, of course, never administered openly, but always secretly and generally in the shape of an ordinary drink – in water, milk or tea. The main thing was that the drink should contain the all-important secret ingredients which were supposed to give it its potency. One of the most commonly used of these ingredients was the juice of a boiled field mouse.

Yet another means employed for the purpose of alluring young men was the following: catch a frog, put it in a box and bury it alive in a bank or dry ditch; when the flesh of the frog withers to the bare skeleton, pick the bones apart and select a certain bone; the next step then was to endeavour to secretly insert this bone in the clothing of the victim with the result that he or she will fall madly in love with the person who had placed the bone there in the first place. The victims of ministrations such as these were not entirely without means of defence, however, for there were a number of measures which could be taken in order to counteract their effect. One particularly useful method was to cut off a bit of hair of a girl in question, burn the hair and feed the ashes to the young man, mixed in with his tea or food.

Another defensive ploy was to cut a bit of cloth out of the girl's dress or a few tassels off her shawl. These stolen bits of material were used to work a spell which had the effect of altering the young man's love and affection to cold hate. These pieces of cloth or tassels had to be procured by stealth, of course, and people often went to great trouble to get them, frequently employing the services of a third party – a middleman – above suspicion.

Dance houses where country dances were being held, wake houses during the hurly burly of wake games, or even a crowded chapel on a Sunday were favourite places for snipping off the cloth or tassels. The women and girls with their long wide skirts and heavy shawls, tasselled and decorated with trimmings were easy targets in any crowded company. Even a girl's hair could be cut unknown to her for they used to wear their hair in flowing tresses down their backs or sometimes in a hanging plait.

In different parts of the country, various herbs and

recipes were used in a variety of ways. Here are a few examples:

In Kerry, a herb called the early purple orchid was used in making a charm for 'coaxing women' as this account states. The charm was made as follows: 'Get ten silk pins, kill a mouse and stick the pins in his body until they get rusty. When the pins are rusty, get a *ballavaun beake* (sort of mushroom) and stick the pins in it and leave then there for three days. Pluck the *Mainglín Meidhreach* and rub the pins to it. Any girl that you stick one of these pins in her clothes will follow you all over the world.'

It is said, of course, that it takes a mother twenty-one years to rear her son but that it only takes a quarter of an hour for a woman to make a fool of him – with or without unnatural means.

A Cork recipe offers a way out for both girls and boys: 'If a girl got the idea that the boy she fancied was not fond of her, then she should boil the excrement of a white gander and give it to him to drink, unknown to him. She could be sure of his love ever after. On the other hand, if the boy thought the girl wasn't fond enough of him, he would boil the excrement of a black chicken and give it to the girl to drink, unknown to her. The girl would hunt the country after him – she'd follow him from this to Bantry Bay after it.'

From Cork to the other end of Ireland – to Raithlin Island, in fact, where Michael J. Murphy, one of Ireland's best known folklore collectors, heard the following account in August 1954:

'I heard of a coax-ee-lorum,' said Michael J.'s informant, 'and I was told in this island, it was true, and I saw it was true. It worked with pistrugs. It was done with an apple.

'They were Protestant boys at the Lower End and the boys from the Upper End used to be going down, and they came home all the way to beyond north Claggan. When they were at their own gate they had to turn back and go to the girls' house and get them out.

'The girls got an apple and peeled a bit, just eased up the skin, and made a cut in the apple and put the pistrugs in the cut and eased the skin back. And the boys were given an apple and ate it and thought nothing of it. But it worked. What they put in, I don't know, but it could be the herb. I just heard they put pistrugs into the cut. They done that with the power of the Devil, a charm. It was done several times on this Island.'

From Rathlin Island in the north we go to Wexford in the south-east. Here is a story noted down by Patrick Kennedy, and published by him in his *Fireside Stories of Ireland*, called *The Love Philtre – A Fact.*

'Nora, a healthy, bouncing young damsel, but no way gifted with beauty, registered a vow that she would be the wife of young Mr Bligh, a "half sir" that lived near. The young fellow always spoke civilly and good-natured-ly to her, but after a year or two's acquaintance, Nora saw no immediate sign of her vow being accomplished.

'She held consultations with adepts in fairy and demon lore, and discovered that the liver of a cat, thoroughly black, white paws excepted, was sovereign in the process of procuring a return of love. Aided by her sister and another woman, researches were made, the cat discovered and slain, with accompaniments which we do not choose to particularise. The liver was then carefully taken out, broiled and reduced to an impalpable powder.

'In a day or two, the gallant was passing by Nora's cottage, and seeing her at the gate, he "put the speak" on her. She, nothing loth, kept up the conversation, and after some further talk, asked might she take the liberty of requesting him to come in and take a cup of tea. He did not think the better of her prudence for making the demand, but felt he couldn't refuse without incivility. So he was set comfortably at table and Nora soon filled his cup from a black teapot, which in addition to some indifferent tea, contained a pinch of the philtre.

'The guest began the banquet with notions and intentions not very complimentary to his entertainer; but when he took up his hat to walk home, he was determined on setting her up as the mistress of his heart and house. It is in the nature of this magic potion that if the dose is not repeated at intervals the effect becomes weaker, and at length ceases altogether. Nora, aware of this, renewed the administration at every visit till his infatuation became such that he announced to his family and relations his immediate marriage with the cabin girl.

'Vain were coaxings, threats, reasonings, etc; and at last the eve of their wedding day arrived.

'Paying a visit to his chamber that happy evening, they were enjoying the most interesting and delightful conversation, when the latch was raised and a party of seven or eight young fellows, armed with good hazel rods, entered and began to lay thousands on his devoted back and shoulders. Nora flung herself between and received a few slight blows; but before they ceased practising on the amorous youth, every bone in his body was sore, and he himself unable to use his arms or legs.

'That was what they wanted. They trundled him into a car and took him home, where he was tended and watched for a month. The drug not being administered all that time, he was amazed when he was able to quit bed that he should ever have been guilty of such an absurdity. So to Nora's remorse for the unholy proceeding was now added chagrin at her want of success.'

THE GLÁM DÍCENN*
PATRICK C. POWER

The poet Aithirne is supposed to have lived at some time about the beginning of the Christian era. He had two sons who became interested in the wife of Conor McNessa, the King of Ulster. It is said that when they made advances towards her, she resisted them and they composed a *glám dícenn* on her which disfigured her face with three blisters. One of these was white, another was red and the third was black. So humiliated was she that she died of shame. When Conor discovered the cause of her death, he raided the dwelling place of the malefactors and put them to death. One is led to speculate as to whether this was actually possible. It could be true that severe trauma could have caused blisters and this lends a semblance of truth to what might appear at first glance merely a naïve legend form olden times.

More celebrated than the story of Aithirne's sons is that of Caeir who was supposedly a king in Connacht in pre-Christian times. Caeir was unfortunate in three things: he had a dissatisfied wife, a nephew in whom his wife was interested, and a knife which he was under strict *geis*, or taboo not to part with. The queen decided to rid herself of her husband and she knew that the infliction of a physical blemish on him would accomplish

---

* From *The Book of Irish Curses*

this, because this disqualified a man from kingship under the old Gaelic laws.

It was considered a serious breach of courtesy and an even more serious loss of face for a ruler to refuse a poet the fee he demanded in ancient Ireland. The queen prevailed on her husband's nephew, Néde, to demand the knife as a reward for a poem, knowing that her husband could not possibly solve the dilemma he found himself in. When Caeir found himself trapped by the nature of Néde's request, he was effectively destroyed. Néde was obliged to compose a *glám dicenn* on him which was as follows:

> *Maile baire gaire Caieur!*
> *combeodutar celtra catha Caeir!*
> *Caeir diba Caeir dira Caeir foro!*
> *fomara fochara Caeir!*

This quatrain is rather obscure but may be translated as follows:

> Evil, death, short life of Caeir;
> May spears of battle destroy Caeir!
> May Caeir perish! may Caeir pay! may it reach Caeir!
> Under rocks and mounds may Caeir be!

What ritual accompanied this malediction is not recorded but three blisters arose on the king's face – red, white and black – which so disfigured him that he fled in shame, leaving both wife and kingdom to Néde. There the story might have concluded had Néde not repented of his conduct in laying a curse on an innocent man. He decided to visit Caeir in his refuge and journeyed in the former king's chariot accompanied by the origin of all the bother – the queen. When they reached Caeir's hiding-place, Néde insisted on coming face to face with him. Caeir died instantly of shame and at the moment of his death a rock nearby exploded, sending a splinter into Néde's eye and killing him at the same moment.

2

Guessing Games and Telling the Future

Human beings spend an enormous amount of time engrossed in one of their favourite inventions: the future. Many of their fears, hopes and despairs are centred on matters that, in the course of things, never happen. Nowhere is this truer than in the area of love. What follows is a selection of ruses employed to counteract the inevitable conclusion that *you just don't know.*

DIVINATION GAMES*

KEVIN DANAHER

Games and pastimes in which divination played a part were sure to be performed in any household which included young people. The best known of these, and the most popular today, is the inclusion of certain objects in the *bairín breac* (the large fruit cake), a ring, a small sil-

---

* From *The Year in Ireland.*

ver coin, a button, a thimble, a chip of wood, and a rag were mixed in with the dough in making the cake, and foretold the finder's future.

The ring meant early marriage, the coin wealth, the button bachelorhood and the thimble spinsterhood while the chip of wood revealed that the finder would be beaten by the marriage partner and the rag meant poverty. Some put in a pea and bean to tell of future poverty and wealth. A little religious medal indicated that the finder would take holy orders or enter a convent.

In some households, the ominous objects were put, not into the cake but into the dish of colcannon or champ which formed the main dish. M. J. Murphy (*At Slieve Gullion's Foot*, p. 45) says:

'A marriage ring was often mixed in the champ. Here boys and girls gathered round a pot on the floor, and armed with big spoons, tried to be the first to get the ring in their mouths. The winner would be married ere next Hallow Eve. This game, however, was most amusing. Little chivalry or decorum was observed in the eagerness to get the ring, and the champ went over hair and eyes and ears as well as into the mouth.'

Sometimes a little circle of withy was used instead of a wedding ring.

Two other games are described in *Journal of the Kildare Archaeological Society*, p. 448, 1908:

'Two hazel-nuts, walnuts, or chestnuts, or even two grains of wheat, were selected and named after some boy and girl who were supposed to be courting. They were then placed side by side on a bar of the grate, or in the turf-ashes, and according as to whether they burned quietly, or jumped apart from one another, so would be the future before them.

'Four plates having been set down on a table, water was poured into one, a ring placed on another, some clay in the third, and in the fourth was placed either some straw, salt or meal. A person would then be blindfolded and led up to the table, and into whichever plate he or she placed their hand, so would their future turn out. The water signified migration, the ring marriage, the clay death, and the fourth plate prosperity. On re-arranging the order of the plates, others would be blindfolded and led up in like manner.'

In County Kerry two beans were named for couples, first heated and then dropped into a vessel of water, with the words:

Píosam, pósam,
Lánamha phóire,
I méisín uisce,
I lár na teine,
Is tá mo lánamha pósta.

(Píosam, pósam,
A pair of beans
In a dish of water

25

In the middle of the fire

And my pair are married.)

If both beans sink at once, then the named pair are sure to marry and live in harmony. If one sinks and one floats, they will not marry, if both float they will marry and quarrel. *Folklore*, 1893, p. 361–2 has a note from Laois by Miss A. Watson which tells of another popular game:

'When we were children Hallow Eve was always an occasion for practising mysterious rites, the end and aim of each being to foretell the future. The first thing always was to get an old iron spoon, filled with lead in scraps; this was held over a hot fire till it melted. Then a key, which *must* be the hall-door key, was held over a tub of cold water, and the hot lead was poured through the wards of the key. The lead cooled in falling through the water, and when it had all settled in the bottom of the tub, the old nurse proceeded to read its surface. I don't know whether there was originally one especial story of the 'willow pattern' description, but I do know that the many I have heard all bore a family likeness. There was always a castle with a tower here, and a narrow window there, and a knight riding to the door to deliver a beautiful lady who was imprisoned there. And of course the lady was the round-eyed child who was listening with bated breath, and who was eventually to marry said knight. (If anyone likes to try the experiment, he will find that the lead falls in wriggles like snakes, with no possible pretensions to any shape or form.)'

This is, of course, a child's version of the game. Usually the leaden shapes were taken to represent the trade or profession of the future husband, a hammer for a smith, a scissors for a tailor and so on. Some said that the key should be taken for the occasion without the owner's consent, others that it should be a widow's door key.

Lady Wilde, in *Ancient Legends of Ireland*, p. 111, describes another divination game:

'Another spell is the building of the house. Twelve couples are taken, each being made of two holly twigs tied together with a hempen thread: these are all named and struck round in a circle in the clay. A live coal is then placed in the centre, and whichever couple catches fire first will assuredly be married. Then the future husband is invoked in the name of the Evil One to appear and quench the flame.

'On one occasion a dead man in his shroud answered the call, and silently drew away the girl from the rest of the party. The fright turned her brain, and she never recovered her reason afterwards. The horror of that apparition haunted her for ever, especially as on November Eve it is firmly believed that the dead really leave their graves and have power to appear amongst the living.'

MARRIAGE DIVINATION*
KEVIN DANAHER

Besides the divination games there were many tricks carried out by individuals and in private to divine marriage prospects.

The County Clare schoolmaster, Brian Merriman, in the long Irish poem *Cúirt an Mheadhon Oidhche* which he wrote towards the end of the eighteenth century, puts into the mouth of one of his female characters an account of the methods which she used in attempts to divine the identity of her future husband, which may be translated thus:

'No trick of which you'd read or hear
At dark of moon, or when it's clear,
At Shrove or Samhain or through the year,
That I've not tried to find my dear!
Under my pillow I've kept all night
A stocking stuffed with apples tight,
For hours a pious fast kept up
Without a thought of bite or sup.
My shift I'd draw against the stream
In hope of my sweetheart to dream.
The stack I'd sweep without avail.
Left in the embers hair and nail.
The flail against the gable laid.

* From *The Year in Ireland.*

Under my bolster put the spade.
My distaff in the oast would lie.
I'd drop spun yarn in the lime-kiln's eye.
Flax seed upon the road I'd fling.
A cabbage head to bed I'd bring.
There is no trick of these I mention
That I've not tried for the Devil's intention!'

All of this young lady's devices were widely known in Ireland. In addition to the apples, the cabbage head and the spade, other things which might be put under the pillow or under the head of the bed to induce a dream of the future partner were *bairin breac*, or the first spoonful of colcannon from the supper dish and the last left on the plate, both put into the girl's left stocking and tied with her right garter, or nine ivy leaves with the words:

Nine leaves I place under my head
to dream of the living and not of the dead,
to dream of the man I am going to wed,
and to see him tonight at the foot of my bed.

The young lady's pious fast was intended to induce thirst, so that she might dream of her future husband offering her a drink of water. A salt herring eaten at bedtime, or heavily salted porridge, or a spoonful of mixed flour, salt and soot were held to be equally effective.

Drawing one's shift against the stream was a preliminary to drying it. Some believed that it should be wrung out on the river bank, on which the figure of the lover will be seen on the opposite bank, or his face reflected on the water. Others said that it must be hung up to dry, and the watching girl would see her future husband turning it during the night. Sometimes a young man would dip and dry his shirt in this way to see his future wife.

'Sweeping the stack' was sweeping around the corn stack with a broom three times in the hope that on the third circuit the future partner would appear or his name be spoken aloud. Another version omits the sweeping and claims that to walk around the stack three times was sufficient.

Hair and nail clippings dropped into the last embers of the fire was another powerful charm to induce a dream of the husband or wife to be. The flail and the spade, essentially masculine implements, were sure to bring a vision of the chosen man, while the *cuigeal*, the distaff from the spinning wheel, placed in the corn-drying kiln would have a like result.

Dropping a ball of woollen thread into the pit of the lime-kiln and winding it back slowly was a sort of fishing. If the thread caught, the girl asked who was holding it, and the voice of the future husband should answer. In another version of this charm the ball of yarn was dropped out of the girl's window. General Vallency, in *Collectanea de Rebus Hibernicis*, xii, p. 460, says that the *Pater Noster* was recited backwards while winding in the wool.

Bravest of all was the girl who made her way to the crossroads as the night wore on and there sprinkled flax seed on the road or laid a *súgán* across it, for at the very hour of midnight her future husband would be stepping across it.

If an apple is peeled in one long strip and the peel allowed to fall upon the ground, it will form the initials of the future husband, and if an apple is eaten before a mirror his face is seen looking over the girl's shoulder. Lady Wilde tells of a tragic sequel to this, in *Ancient Legends of Ireland*, p. 110:

'And a lady narrates that on 1 November her servant rushed into the room and fainted on the floor. On recovering, she said that she had played a trick that night in the name of the Devil before the looking-glass; but what she had seen she dared not speak of, though the remembrance of it would never leave her brain, and she knew the shock would kill her. They tried to laugh her out of her fears, but the next night she was found quite dead, with her features horribly contorted, lying on the floor before the looking-glass, which was shivered to pieces.'

If the face is washed but not dried before going to bed, the lover will appear in a dream, proffering a towel.

Ashes, raked from the fire and spread evenly over the hearthstone may be found in the morning to bear footprints or other significant marks, while if a little flour is spread smoothly on a large plate or dish, and a live snail

31

dropped on it, the creature's progress through the flour will spell out the initials or letters which carry a message of hope or disappointment for future marital bliss.

A number of small scraps of paper were each marked with a letter of the alphabet, and these were floated face downwards on a basin of water. In the morning they should be found to have sunk to the bottom, and those which have turned over to show the letters will show the initials or spell the name of the future spouse.

A daring girl might take a mouthful of water, and holding it in the mouth without swallowing, creep close to the door or window of a neighbour's house and listen until the name of a young unmarried man was mentioned in the conversation by somebody within, when by virtue of the charm this youth would become her husband. A grain of wheat held between the teeth was believed by some to be equally potent.

Three stalks of corn pulled from the stack at the dead of night could also tell their tale. The first two were discarded, but the state of the third ear would surely reveal, by its form and size, how rich and how handsome would be the destined husband or wife.

A head of cabbage, pulled up by the root gave much information on the crucial marriage option. A. J. Pollock, in *Ulster Folklife*, p. 62, 1960, gives a version from County Down of this very widespread custom:

'The girls were blindfolded and sent out in pairs, hand in hand, to the garden or field and told to pull the first cabbage they found. It size and shape – whether it was big or small, straight or crooked – would indicate the shape and stature of their future spouse. If much earth adhered to the root they would have plenty of money; if there was only a little they would be poor. The taste of the "custoc", i.e., the heart, would tell his temper and disposition, according to whether it was sweet or bitter. Finally the "runts" or stems were hung above the door; each was given a number and the name of a boy friend, for example Barney might be the name given to the third runt. If Barney was the third person to enter the house on the night, this was considered to be a good omen.'

Other versions go further and say that if the young man indicated in the charm can by some means be induced to eat part of the same cabbage head, he will inevitably lead the girl to the altar.

Another charm from County Down, but widely known elsewhere, is given by the same writer, p. 63:

'If none of these charms worked you could always try to "winnow three wechts of nothing", the wecht being the skin of a winnowing tray. You had to go alone to a barn, open both doors and take them off their hinges. This was important, for the Being that would appear might otherwise shut the doors and do you harm. You then took the wecht and went through the motions of winnowing corn in a strong wind. This was repeated three times, and on the third occasion an apparition would pass through the barn, in at the "windy" door and out through the other.

The face would be that of your future husband, and the clothes he wore and the tools he carried would tell you both his occupation and station in life.'

A similar charm, to be carried out by a young man, is given in the *Journal of the Kildare Archaeological Society*, p. 449, 1908:

'A boy would go to a barn and sow oats along its floor, in the name of the Devil, from one end to the other. Having done that, he would go to the door, open it, and expect to see the fetch of his future wife standing outside. Instances have been known where, in place of the fetch, a coffin appeared, and this foretells to the beholder that he will not be alive on that night twelve-month.'

R. H. Buchanan (*Ulster Folklife*, p. 68, 1963) gives a further charm from County Down:

'In many parts of Co. Down salt was used in another way. Here the girl would sprinkle salt on the four corners of the bed and repeat the following verse:

> Salt, salt I salt thee
> In the name of God in unity.
> If I'm for a man or a man for me
> In my first sleep may I see him,
> The colour of his hair, the clothes he'll wear
> The day he weds with me.

Marriage divination by means of little ladders and spinning wheels, as noted on St Brighid's Eve, was also, and perhaps more generally, practised on Hallow's E'en, which was above all others the proper season for such activities. Rose Shaw, in *Charleton's Country*, p. 57, refers to this custom in the Clogher Vallery of county Tyrone:

'Also they made wee ladders with rushes cut in Three Counties Hollow, and they would hang the ladders above their beds that night – a sure way for a girl to see "himself" walk up the ladder in her dreams.'

Before leaving the subject we may mention two others, although this does not exhaust the full catalogue. Both are from County Longford and are given by Cáir Ní Bhrádaigh in *Béaloideas*, p. 268-9, 1936:

'Put three knots on the left garter, and at every knot say:

> This knot, this knot, this knot I see,
> The thing I never saw yet.
> To see my love in his array
> And what he walks in every day,
> And what his occupation,
> This night may I in my dream see.
> And if my love be clad in green,
> His love for me it is well seen.
> And if my love be clad in grey,
> His love for me is far away.
> And if my love is clad in blue,
> His love for me is very true.

'Go to bed, place the knotted garter under your pillow, and you will see your future husband in a dream.

'Cut nine stalks of yarrow with a black-handled knife. When all are gone to bed say:

> Good morrow, good morrow, my pretty yarrow!
> I pray before this time tomorrow
> You will tell who my true love shall be.
> The clothes that he wears, and the name that he
>   bears,
> And the day that he'll come and wed me.'

The black-handled knife in this last example is a well-known charm against fairies and other uncanny visitors. Such protection was not unwelcome, for in all these divination charms there is, in tradition, an uncomfortable sense of dabbling with unseen and potentially malevolent powers.

Some death divination was practised too. A note in the *County Louth Archaeological Journal*, 1910, p. 323, reads:

'The above customs closely resemble the following one still practised in Farney and probably other parts of Ireland: On Hallow-eve night each member of the family gets an ivy leaf without spot or stain and immerses it in a glass or cup of water where it is allowed to stand over night. In the morning, if the leaf is still spotless, the person who set it in the water is sure of life at least until that day twelve months, but if the leaf is found spotted in the morning the person it represents will surely die during the ensuing year. Such, at least, is the belief. Some leaves undoubtedly become spotted when allowed to stand some time in water, probably owing to bacteriological causes.'

Another is given by R. H. Buchanan in *Ulster Folklife*, 1963, p. 68:

'Another Mourne custom, which was also recorded a century ago in Armagh, was to fill a thimble full of salt and turn it upside-down on a plate. "Stacks" of salt were made for each person, left overnight, and if one should have fallen by next morning the person so named would die within the next twelve months.'

LOVE DREAMS*
LADY WILDE

The girl who wishes to see her future husband must go out and gather certain herbs in the light of the full moon of the new year, repeating this charm:

Moon, moon, tell unto me
When my true love I shall see?
What fine clothes am I to wear?
How many children shall I bear?

---

* From *Quaint Irish Customs and Superstitions*.

For if my love comes not to me
Dark and dismal my life shall be.

Then the girl, cutting three pieces of clay from the sod with a black-hafted knife, carries them home, ties them up in the left stocking with the right garter, places the parcel under her pillow, and dreams a true dream of the man she will marry and of her future fate.

HASTE TO THE WEDDING*
KEVIN DANAHER

And all sorts of signs and portents were observed on the wedding day. A fine day meant luck especially if the sun shone on the bride; a day of rain foretold hardship. It was unlucky to marry on a Saturday, and those who married in harvest would spend all their lives gathering. A man should always be the first to wish joy to the bride, never a woman, although we hear of cases where jealous or spiteful women tried to bring bad luck on a marriage by forestalling the man. It was lucky to hear a cuckoo on the wedding morning, or to see three magpies. To meet a funeral on the road meant bad luck, and if there was a funeral on that day, the wedding party on the way to the groom's house, or to or from the church always took a different road. The wedding day was a big day for the whole townland, and nothing should be allowed to cast a shadow over it.

---

* From *In Ireland Long Ago.*

3

Matchmaking

Matchmaking, or marriage by arrangement, was, as we see from the account below, not as strict and binding a matter as is sometimes thought.

THE MATCH*

KEVIN DANAHER

In some places there were recognised matchmakers who – for a consideration – were prepared to act as go-between. More usually the matter was arranged by the parents or friends of the young couple meeting at fair or market and repairing to the back room of the village pub to thresh the matter out, with long discussions on the merits of the boy or girl and much argument over the dowry and other details of the marriage settlement. In our part of the country, however, the first steps were taken by some friends of the young man visiting the girl's house and 'drawing down' the match with her parents. The favourite time for such visits was 'between Big and

---

* From *In Ireland Long Ago.*

Little Christmas', with a view to a wedding the following Shrove. In a farming community it was necessary that there should be economic and social parity between the boy and girl, hence the matchmaking, and hence the long discussion on the dowry and the man's expectations. If he had the grass of twenty cows it was understood that the 'fortune' should be greater than he might expect if he had the grass of only ten. It was expected, too, that the friends of the girl would visit the man's farm and see the quality of the land and the evidence of his husbandry. 'Walking the land' is what that was called, and the visiting party must be well entertained in the young man's home – any lack of hospitality or any sign of meanness counted heavily against the success of the venture. Tales are told of matches made without the young people's knowledge, but more usually the parties mainly concerned had the right of refusal if the match did not appeal to them, and frequently there already was an understanding between them, and the friends who came to make the match knew of it.

In the old days, before the Famine, people married young, and a young couple expected to be guided and advised by their elders both before and after the marriage. Indeed, neither the man nor woman reached full status in the rural community until they were married. The unmarried were still 'boys' and 'girls' even up to their old age, and a married woman of twenty-one had a much more important position in life than a spinster of fifty.

The same held good for the men. All this was acceptable when people did marry young; to see a young married man advised and guided by his parents was edifying, but as the nineteenth century went on, and marriages were entered upon later and later in life, the sight of a 'boy' of close on fifty being ordered about by a doddering old parent was by no means a reassuring spectacle. In one such case an old friend of mine tried to persuade an elderly woman that her only son, aged forty-nine, might be better settled down in life. 'Yerra, hould your whist!' was her reply. 'Wouldn't another tin years be great hardening in him?'

Matchmaking did not always run smoothly. There was the case, not a hundred miles from the Kerry border, where the boy and girl were agreed, and the boy's family were all for the match, but her old father was a tough customer and hard to pin down. Three times the match seemed to be made, and three times broken by his obstinacy, until, at length, the boy's mother called on the parish priest to tell him that everything was arranged and the day set. 'Tell me, ma'am,' said the priest, 'how ever did you get round old Johnny?'

'Well, to tell you the truth, father, we told a few of the boys to go over and fire a few shots outside the house to show him that we were in earnest.' There are always ways and means to smooth the course of love.

4

Fairy Love

The fairies, believed to be descended from the original, mythical inhabitants of Ireland, lived (or live) life for enjoyment. Sex inevitably came into the equation, and the fairies didn't (or don't) balk at making use of mortals for their own amorous ends.

FAIRY CLOTHES AND APPEARANCE*
CAROLYN WHITE

Naturally each fairy dresses according to his or her taste, but there are general styles, fashionable now for thousands of years. Ladies prefer shimmering silver gauze for dining at home, and white shifts when travelling abroad in mortal realms – white shifts against the night blackness being known to produce startling effects on mortal sensibilities.

At home fairy ladies and gentlemen enjoy adorning themselves with the treasures of the earth, especially with diamonds and pearls. Somewhere about their per-

---

* From *A History of Irish Fairies*.

sons lies a fillip of gold, on a cap, perhaps, or a hem of a dress. Sea fairies have an easier access to pearls; but land fairies prefer necklaces made from serpents' scales, which they have had to import from England since St Patrick chased the snakes from Ireland.

Of course, a great deal of red is worn by fairies as well as displayed in their homes, for red is the colour of magic, and a great deal of green, for is that not the colour of the fields and the woods and of Ireland itself? Therefore red caps are all the rage in male fairy circles, well-fitting green garments eternally in style. On occasion fairies do sport about in foxglove caps, but mortals have been too quick to cry, 'fairy', every time they spy the fox-glove and so have falsely attributed diminutive size to the good, but not always so wee, people.

Fairy men and women are as perfectly proportioned as Greek statues, but not so heavy of limb. The bodies of either sex display magnificent features, but mortal writ-ers prefer to dwell upon the female form and hence to devote their descriptions to the fairer sex. Although a few brunettes exist among the fairy court (perhaps from intermarriages with the dark-haired Celts), most ladies have fair hair which would be a disgrace if it did not del-icately sweep the ground. Such women have a rather sleepy look, with languid bodily movements and a slow feline voluptuousness. Hot-blooded women, they think nothing of ravishing a man in an evening's sport or infusing his blood with a fierce war lust. Yet despite the exquisite virtues of brunette and blonde fairy women alike, fairy men have, for centuries, eyed the mortal form, as have the fairy women themselves despite the fine qualities of their men. Perhaps after a thousand-year acquaintance they desire novelty. But more likely, fairies love mortal men and women because overflowing with love and rejoicing in all beauty, they have the immortal strength to embrace all that is beautiful of both races.

Oftentimes fairies appear before mortals in ancient deformed shapes. But when fairies come to the mortal realms for love, their clothes are tasteful and their bodies straight. They travel abroad most often in troops, and then little is seen of their fine array and splendidly proportioned bodies. They cover themselves with such swirls of dust and straw that not a gold buckle nor a red cap can be seen. A shrill sound like buzzing thrills the air as they storm by with such force that a mortal, knocked down abruptly and dazed of sense, remembers nothing but a great buzzing wind. To see fairies in all their regalia one must be escorted to fairyland itself.

BEAUTIFUL WOMEN AND NURSING MOTHERS*

CAROLYN WHITE

Fairies claim all beautiful things (including human) as their own and they always need fine, strong women to nurse the stolen young. Therefore, beautiful women and nursing mothers frequently take up residence in fairy-land.

Many a high-spirited girl climbed the mountains never to return; many a colleen, gazing down into a lake, sang so soulfully of her heart's desire that she spent the next seven years looking upward and singing from a sea palace below. The fairies gather beauty as a young girl wild flowers; and they as willingly discard them once the bloom is gone. The immortal ones have no compassion for the messy decay and death of the human race. They require lovely women in their prime; some just for an evening (their forms seemingly lying abed) to dance with the wild king Fionvarra; some for the allotted seven years to wed and dance each night with fairy chiefs in impassioned embraces.

The intensity of fairy life ravishes them, and they return home to the mortal realm as shrivelled, old hags. Some return home with no toes, having danced them away. Yet despite their deformities their eyes flame and

* From *A History of Irish Fairies.*

45

their voices quiver with longing. Although mortals respect them as grand fairy doctors, they shrug off the honours; when humans offer companionship they head for the quiet places where fairies are reputed to be.

Humans are made of strange yearning stuff; they always desire what has passed or what will never be. Therefore the fairies, secure in eternity and awake to the present, have difficulty understanding their mortal brethren. Like mortals they are ravished by desire; but it never withers them. Rather, it tunes them finely like a well-used lyre which plays sweeter the more it is stroked. When a mortal woman desires so that her very marrow aches, she is most like the fairies, and they embrace her as kin in Tír-na-n-Óg. A young girl once died of desire for fairy music. To honour her passion the fairies caused delicate roses to grow on her grave. Most women die when seized with longing for fairy things; but a few, a very rare few, overcome death by desire, and thus remain young and eternal among the *sidhe.*

Fairy interest in nursing mothers is of a much more practical nature; consequently their term of residence is of shorter duration. Fairies abduct them to nurse stolen, mortal children and sometimes fairy children whose mothers are sickly after the birth. At night they return home to feed their own, thus giving a husband an opportunity to reclaim his wife. After sunset the stolen woman appears about the house, sometimes as a venomous snake, sometimes as a wrinkled hag in a pall; but the devoted husband braces himself, saying never a word, and gives her something to eat so that she may refuse the fatal fairy food. Eventually she will regain her own form to give suck to the child. If she falls asleep on the third night, all is well. The man quickly stretches a red string across the threshold to prevent the fairies' entry; then, in the name of God, he sprinkles her with holy water. She will then assume her true form and remain at home as blithe as ever.

There are many methods of reclaiming a stolen woman. Some are quite complicated since beautiful women, unlike nursing mothers, are not allowed to return home. One must, therefore, go to the fairies. Since it is nearly impossible to catch the fairies napping at home, a husband or lover had best discover them when they travel abroad. Sometimes it takes months of searching hills and graveyards until they are found. But if he is intent in his pursuit, he carries a black-hafted knife and waits for the troop to ride out at night. Since fairy troops travel screened by whirlwind and mist, it is nearly impossible to distinguish one rider from another, yet the determined man always manages to do so. At the first rider that passes he stabs hard and once only, for a second thrust would undo the harm. The mist about the troop vanishes at once; the woman then clearly appears. By force he pulls her from her horse, drawing her close to him in a ring made of holy water, which the fairies dare not transgress. Within the ring he anoints her with chosen herbs gathered near the fairy fort. Protected by the herbs she can safely return home. But if the man slips up on any of these steps, he will lose his woman forever.

Since fairies generally leave a replacement for those women (especially nursing mothers) they abduct on a temporary basis, a man may be fortunate enough to have an image substituted for the true wife. If this is the case, his task is simple. While the false form sleeps, he unfastens her girdle and tosses it into the fire, making sure to bury the pin that bound it under the earth. The false form will vanish; the true return; and the man need never concern himself with black-hafted knives and fairy riders. As long as the pin lies safely buried, the flesh-and-blood woman can live contentedly at home with her man.

Women with husbands most often return. Not only are husbands most skilled in procuring their escape but married women do not acclimatise properly to fairyland. They persist in their previous attachments. Unmarried girls, however, need think only of themselves, and being purer in intent, adjust more easily to fairy custom.

THE LIANHAN SHEE*

CAROLYN WHITE

The lianhan shee is a fairy woman of dreadful power, for she seeks the love and dominion of mortal men. Only one lianhan shee exists and she is more a force than a woman. Yet each fairy woman who loves ('Lianhan Shee' means the love fairy) becomes one with her; and for the mortal man who longs for her she is the one and only. When the lianhan shee appears, nothing else exists. She does not trifle with emotions; all who love her live for her and exult in their desire which frequently destroys them. The more suffering she inflicts the dearer she becomes to them. The more they desire her the more she eludes them, her absence like a fine chain pulling them towards her.

Connla the Bold saw a woman upon a hill who called to him and offered herself and eternal beauty in the Land of the Living. Although all heard her words, no one but he saw her. Desirous he reached towards her, but she threw him an apple to stay his pursuit. For a month he ate of nothing but the ever-sustaining apple; no other food nor drink appealed. No thoughts but of her concerned him. He forgot his people and ignored the words of his friends. And when the woman sent him a crystal boat, he joyfully leaped at it, sailing towards her with

* From *A History of Irish Fairies.*

never a backward look. Connla was never seen again, but assuredly now, as always, he enjoys his love in the Land of the Heart's Desire.

A fairy woman visited Angus Óg by dream. Each night for a year she played silver music for him on a harp. When he reached towards her she vanished; but when he lay still, she sat by his bedside and lulled him to sleep. At the year's end her visits stopped and Angus grew ill with love-longing. Physicians found no physical ailments; only the presence of his beloved could cure him. Finally, after endless searching, he found her in the shape of a swan; and since he could not live without her, he too became a bird. The music they made as they flew rang so sweetly that all who heard it fell asleep for three days and three nights.

An impatient mistress, the lianhan shee creates such desire in her lovers that they overcome all obstacles to embrace her. She never yields to them in mortal lands, but insists on their meeting in Tir-na-n-Óg, so that men must pass through death to enjoy her. All the great poets and musicians loved her; almost all died young. She rent their hearts and in their blood-agony began song. The more they sang the more their bodies withered; until they sang for her forever.

No one has ever described the lianhan shee. Perhaps each stricken man jealously guards his love and fears the world's knowledge of her. But more likely no mortal can describe her; for ineffable as desire itself, the lianhan shee eludes all attempts to limit her glory. She may select her lovers from our realm, but she never allows her story to remain long on their mortal lips.

THE UNION OF MORTALS AND FAIRIES*
CAROLYN WHITE

When a fairy woman falls in love with a mortal, he holds all power over her until he succumbs to her charms. Once he loves, he offers body and soul to her to use as she wills. She consumes him; he joyfully submits. So it is, in more recent times, that a mortal, surrendering to his passion, dies of it. But in the days of the heroes, men and women were equal to fairy love; and since they were granted immortality they still must be celebrating their love to this day. Oisín was a vigorous lover of a fairy woman for three hundred years until he returned to the mortal realm and died. The great warrior Connla still enjoys his fairy lover.

It is small wonder that fairies no longer raid the mortal realm for husbands and brides. Few, if any, of us could endure the strength of their embrace. Yet some still do; and the children of such a union, half-mortal, half-divine, have a passionate nature, given alternately to moody and vengeful fits and long periods of seeming indolence which erupt abruptly into violent emotions.

* From *A History of Irish Fairies.*

Mortals find these halflings difficult to live with; and they themselves prefer solitude to human contact. Always dissatisfied they wander the hill and converse with unseen spiritual beings.

Perhaps their fretfulness is due to an immortal spirit's struggle against entrapment within a corruptible body, for, regrettably, they inherit one parent's mortality. Their divine nature makes them impatient with their human limits and hence wild and angry. Perhaps they purposely destroy their bodies so that their souls will the sooner re-enter the fairy kingdom. Surely they are not made for this world, but are only passing time amongst us until they can return to fairyland.

Such contrary beings relinquish complacency and comfort and are fitful at their work, sometimes absorbed thoroughly in herding or fishing or housekeeping, often indifferent to all but the magic of the hills. Fairy music is in their blood, fairy song upon their lips; without having studied the art or memorised a line they know all the music of the *sidhe* and sing it effortlessly. Their bodies are as beautiful as their songs for all inherit the perfect features and well-proportioned forms of fairyland's creatures. Their eyes are always fiery, their limbs dove-white, taut and desirable. Like hybrid flowers, they are brilliant in colour, bold in form, painfully intense and short-lived.

5

Proverbs, Sayings, Quotations

Who wants action when you've got words? Well, almost everybody really. But in the meantime, here is a selection of words devoted to the two sexes and their mutual doings.

PROVERBS AND SAYINGS*

BEAUTY

Beauty is only skin deep but nobody wants to be drowned.

A pot was never boiled by beauty.

A blind man is no judge of beauty.

If you have no beauty within you, you'll not perceive it.

---

* From Padraic O'Farrell's *Gems of Irish Wisdom: Irish Proverbs and Sayings*

It's the gem that cannot be owned which is the most beautiful.

The beauty of a chaste woman causes bitter words.

Elegance and beauty are the same thing when there's a man after them.

Always make sure she looks beautiful before breakfast as well as after dinner.

LOVE

Love is blind but the neighbours see through it.

A lad's best friend is his mother until he's the best friend of a lassie.

If she pleases the eye she'll please the heart.

Love is like stirabout, it must be made fresh every day.

Love at first sight often happens in the twilight.

If you live in my heart you live rent-free.

Old coals are easiest kindled.

After the settlement comes love.

If you love her in *giobals* (rags) your love will last.

There's little love until there's a fight.

Jarbles (rags) drop off quicker than tift (fine clothes).

Sheeps' eyes don't see beyond the settle.

Love is not an impartial judge.

Wiggy (light) turf burns bright but not for long.

If she has a mind of her own there won't be many with a mind for her.

Never cross a woman who has been crossed in love.

Wait till you're eighteen to marry and don't be spoiling your growth.

Love cools quickly.

A flicker that warms is better than a blaze that burns.

A broken heart is a broken promise.

Weakening sight means weakening love.

If that fellow doesn't soon get a woman he'll be getting his thrills at the offerings.

Every thrush thinks her mate sings the sweetest.

What's nearest the heart is nearest the lips.

Once you break the ice it won't be long till you can lift the water.

Love is intoxicating. It pleases at first and then sends its victims reeling.

Love is like sun to a flower – it invigorates the strong but wilts the weak.

If a man is in love he is no judge of beauty but when love wears off he'll tell a woman about her warts.

MAN

The man of the house needs three meals a day and four grouses.

Men are like bagpipes: no sound comes from them till they're full.

A man is a man when his woman is a woman.

A sea wind changes less often than the mind of a weak man.

Greatness in a man knows modesty.

A man's fame lasts longer than his life.

Every man to his own taste.

A man works hard for success and then squanders his time talking about it.

No man can prosper without his woman's leave.

WOMAN

She mightn't be much good to boil a pot of spuds but she'd look lovely carrying them to the table.

Women would drive you mad but the asylum would be a cold place without them.

A dishonest woman cannot be kept in and an honest one won't.

There's nothing more vicious than a woman's temper except, maybe, a woman's tongue.

The foolish woman knows the foolish man's faults.

A jealous woman would make trouble between two breast bones.

There's nothing makes the windows (eyes) open like a fine doorful of a woman.

A whistling woman and a crowing hen,
Will bring bad luck to the house they're in.

I wouldn't like to be hanging by the neck since she was thirty.

The heat is often far back in the woman that's forward.

Only shyness or shame prevents a woman from refusing a man.

Man to the hill, woman to the shore,
Boy to the mill, youth to the whore.

It's as hard to see a woman crying as it is to see a bare-footed duck.

It is not the most beautiful woman who has the most sense.

Everything dear is every woman's fancy.

Avoid the woman that has too many nicks in her horn.

A woman without is one who has neither child nor pipe.

Never be in a court or a castle without a woman to make your excuse.

The weak grip of a woman holds tighter than a vice.

A Tyrone woman will never buy a rabbit without a head for fear it's a cat.

A woman and a child are like a goat. If they're not in trouble, they're coming out of it.

It takes a woman to outwit the Devil.

You'd want to be up early to catch a woman out and you'd want to be up late to catch her in.

An inch makes a world of difference when it's in a woman's nose.

Some women are like a Kilmallock fire – little warmth in them.

Wherever there are women there is talking and wherever there are geese there's cackling.

Where comes a cow, there follows a woman,
Where comes a woman, there follows trouble.

A bad woman drinks much of her own buttermilk.

Let her rant and rave as long as the sun is high and as long as she's loving, close and tender when the sun sets.

Like Irish wolves, Irish women bark at their own shadows.

A woman who looks at the window is edgy,
A woman who gazes into the fire is worried.

She's the heart of the roll,
If she gives you a roll;
Leave her back in the Zoo
If she won't give you two.   *Dublin rhyme*

Quotations*

Compliments

Won't you come into the garden? I would like my roses
to see you.

Richard Brinsley Sheridan

Love

Be wise, be wise, and do not try
How he can court, or you be won;
For love is but discovery;
When that is made, the pleasure's done.

Thomas Southerne

Love, an' please your Honour, is exactly like war, in this,
that a soldier, though he has escaped three weeks complete o' Saturday night, may nevertheless be shot
through his heart on Sunday morning.

Lawrence Sterne

When one is in love one begins to deceive oneself. And
one ends by deceiving others.

Oscar Wilde

---

* From Sean Sheehan's *Dictionary of Irish Quotations*.

Love loves to love love. Nurse loves the new chemist. Constable 14A loves Mary Kelly. Gerty MacDowell loves the boy that has the bicycle. M. B. loves a fair gentleman. Li Chi Han lovey up kissy Cha Pu Chow. Jumbo, the elephant, loves Alice, the elephant.

James Joyce

But then all love seemed to be blighted in Ireland, in another deadly kind of famine. Even the words used for the progression of courtship and love are diminishing and unsympathetic, and make the whole business of love and tenderness seem pathetic, ridiculous, so that the effects and states of being in love become matters for concealment. The first kindling of sexual interest, the recognition of anyone of the opposite sex as being special, is called 'having a notion of' and is regarded as a foolish state. Infatuation, or the bloom state of being-in-love, is called 'astray in the head'.

Polly Devlin

SEX

What is virtue but the Trades Unionism of the married?

George Bernard Shaw

... and how he kissed me under the Moorish wall and I thought well as well him as another and then I asked him with my eyes to ask again yes and then he asked me would I yes to say yes my mountain flower and first I put my arms around him yes and drew him down to me so he could feel my breasts all perfume yes and his heart was going like mad and yes I said yes I will Yes.

James Joyce

To her cool mind it had sometimes seemed that the initial expression of tenderness to someone who was – however adored – a stranger, would be difficult to the point of impossibility. It had never occurred to her that the danger of passion might lie not in its novelty but in its naturalness.

Kate O'Brien

During the intervals (between dances) the Devil is busy; yes, very busy, as sad experience proves, and on the way home in the small hours of the morning, he is busier still.

A statement on all-night dances, by Irish bishops,
Irish Catholic, *23 December 1933*

It's rather like teaching swimming from a book without ever having got wet oneself.

Tim Pat Coogan (describing the Catholic Church's rulings on matters of sexual morality)

63

SIN

A flushed young man came from a gap of a hedge and after him came a young woman with wild nodding daisies in her hand. The young man raised his cap abruptly: the young woman abruptly bent and with slow care detached from her light skirt a clinging twig.

Father Conmee blessed both gravely and turned a thin page of his breviary. *Sin.*

James Joyce

6

Poems

Poets sing of ...? That's right – love. But love covers a lot of territory. Below is a series of love poems translated from the Irish by Brendan Kennelly.*

KATE OF GORNAVILLA

Have you been in Gornavilla
Have you seen in Gornavilla
The gay girl with golden hair
Sweet Kate of Gornavilla?

Whiter than the placid swan
Or the snow on the bending bough,
Her kiss as soft as the dew of dawn,
Dear Kate of Gornavilla.

Her song surpasses the young thrush
Or the blackbird in the whitethorn bush;

---

* From Brendan Kennelly's *Love of Ireland: Poems from the Irish.*

Like a ship in sail on a buoyant wave
Is Kate of Gornavilla.

SHE

She
White flower of the blackberry
Sweet flower of the raspberry
Pure herb of beauty
    Blesses the sight of my eyes

She
Heart-pulse and blood-secret
Sweet flower of the apple
Hot sun in cold weather
    Between Christmas and Easter.

HAPPY THE MAN

Happy the man with a lover
In a long-prowed boat
High on the black wave
Leaving the dead land behind
As a risen man
Will quit the grave.

A LOVE-SONG

Such a heart!
Should he leave, how I'd miss him.
Jewel, acorn, youth.
Kiss him!

THE SON OF THE KING OF MOY

The son of the King of Moy
Found a girl in a green dell,
Of the rich abounding fruit
She gave him his fill.

ETAIN

Who will sleep with Etain tonight?
That's still unknown.
One thing is certain though –
Etain won't sleep alone.

HOW GLAD ARE THE SMALL BIRDS

How glad are the small birds
    That rise and sing on one bough;
How near to each other! How far
    Is my love from me now!

White as new milk, sweet as the fiddle,
    Bright as the summer sun
Is she. Dear God in heaven,
    Free me from pain!

KISSES

Keep your kiss, young girl,
    Away with you tonight,
In your kiss I find no taste
    Though your teeth are white.

I kissed a girl for love.
    Sweeter taste I'll never find
In any woman's kiss
    Till time is out of mind.

Until the graceful son of God
    Makes that girl pass my way,
I shall love none, old or young,
    Let her kiss taste how it may.

THE BLACKTHORN PIN

Sweet red-lipped girl, for many years
    You have been loved by men.
Your cloak should bear a golden brooch
    And not a blackthorn pin.

O graceful girl, just to all,
    Whom none could ever win
Why should your yellow cloak show but
    A blackthorn pin?

Wear it then! It is your secret
    And will not be told:
Give the blackthorn pin another hour;
    Then raise the gold.

THE INDIFFERENT MISTRESS

She is my love
Though she makes my life a hell,
Dearer, though she makes me sick,
Than one who would make me well.

She is my dear
Who has reduced me to a slave,

She'd never let one sigh for me
Or lay a stone on my grave.

She is my treasure
Whose eye is stern with pride,
She'd never put an arm under my head
Or lie at my side.

She is my secret
Who won't speak a word to me,
Who won't listen to anything under the sun
Or turn an eye to me.

My plight is sad.
To a lonely death I move.
She who spurns me, only she
Can be my love.

HATE GOES JUST AS FAR AS LOVE

Woman full of hate for me
    Do you not recall the night
When we together, side by side,
    Knew love's delight?

If you remembered woman, how,
    While the sun lost its heat,

You and I grew hot –
      But why repeat?

Do you recall my lips on yours,
      Soft words you said,
And how you laid your curving arm
      Under my head?

Or do you remember, O sweet shape,
      How you whispered passionately
That God Almighty had never made
      A man like me?

I gave all my heart to you,
      Gave all, yet could not give enough;
Now, I've your hate. O skin like flowers,
      This hate goes just as far as love.

If a man believes he loves a woman
      And that she loves him too,
Let him know one thing for certain –
      It is not true.

RECONCILIATION

Do not torment me, woman,
  Let our two minds be as one,
Be my mate in my own land
  Where we may live till life is done.

Put your mouth against my mouth
  You whose skin is fresh as foam,
Take me in your white embrace
  And let us love till kingdom come.

Slender, graceful girl, admit
  Me soon into your bed,
Discord, pain will disappear
  When we stretch there side by side.

For your sweet sake, I will ignore
  Every girl who takes my eye,
If it's possible, I implore
  You do the same for me.

As I have given from my heart
  Passion for which alone I live,
Let me now receive from you
  The love you have to give.

THE MIDNIGHT COURT
BRIAN MERRIMAN*

This is an extract from Merriman's famous Irish poem translated by Cosslett Ó Cuinn. A young girl rebukes the men of Ireland for their amorous shortcomings.

'Shame on you males who, sonless, stand
And do not answer the demand
While women swarm on sea and land,
Sleek buxom fillies fit for stud,
All young hot healthy flesh and blood,
While others suffer from the slump,
Thin, listless without breast or rump,
Or slim and stately once, grow plump.
'Tis sad to think they'll never marry
Or have a healthy child to carry,
'Tis sad to think they'll never swell
In belly and in breasts as well!
Most of them wait there eagerly
Yet, bless them, oh so patiently;
Speak but the word and you will see
Them drop like fruit from the tree ...

'... I have in these my travels too
Met women in their hundreds who,

---

* From Brian Merriman's *The Midnight Court: A New Translation* by Cosslett Ó Cuinn.

Were they but asked, would gladly mate;
I am, like them, quite desperate
Yet, like them I say "no", not "yes"
To spinsterhood and childlessness
Alas, shall sadness ne'er surcease
For gladness, gaiety and peace,
Must gloom and misery fill the night
Spent without sleep or sweet delight.
Without soft peace to shed its balm;
To be condemned as I now am
To tumble in a tepid bed
And struggle with my thoughts instead.
Hear, gracious lady, and redress
The grievances which we express,
We Irishwomen must confess
If the men go on the way they do,
Then we, the weaker sex, must woo,
Or start to capture and pursue!
When they to thoughts of wedlock wake
They're creatures that no girls would take,
Old, worn-out wrecks whose strength is shed
And not worth going with to bed.

'Through youth's rash heat sometimes I own
Exceptions – one in seven – are known
Yet boys whose beards have scarcely grown
Will never choose the girl they wed
For being cultured or well bred,
Or for her figure or her face,

Nor yet, because with easy grace,
She suits her charm with actions fit
Whether she stand or walk or sit.
They go for those most over-dressed
And those who paint their faces best,
Some ugly blonde or dark brown hag,
Who has no charm of which to brag
Except a well-filled money bag.

'It pricks my heart and sends a train
Of puzzling problems through my brain.
I'm sick and worn with all the strain,
Sobs tear me while the tears rain.
I see the sturdy, healthy blade,
Young, manly, handsome and well made,
The gay, the gentle and the kind,
The men of sense, the wise of mind,
Those who know how and when to act
Who show unerring grace and tact,
The men determined and efficient
In all things formidably proficient
At this one point prove insufficient
See then the women whose persistence
Has made such men give up resistance!
Each, for the rest of his existence,
Condemned to cherish with his life
Some elderly or witless wife.
A slut whose head is full of nits
And stops and starts and pets and fits.

75

There in ill-tempered ease she sits
Yet she finds time to snoop and lurk
And give long lectures on the work
That he must do and she may shirk.
He's caught a tartar and a turk.
And I too find it most unfair,
What should be mine has gone to her.
Ochón! That ill-bred wether there,
That old ewe with the young-lamb air
With unwashed feet and uncombed hair
Wedded tonight, that burns and breaks me,
What's wrong with me that no one takes me?

'I'm better looking far than she,
I'm neat and trim and mannerly,
Yet no one falls in love with me.
My lips may well display the row
Of pearl-white teeth which my smiles show,
I have a pretty face I know,
My eyes are bright, my brow like snow,
My eyes are grey, my waving hair
Coils in thick tresses rich and rare,
My chin and cheek unblemished shine,
Frank modesty's in every line.
My hands and fingers, throat and bosom
Win beauty prizes and can't lose 'em.
Although small-boned, light as a feather
No match-stick knees knock I together
My waist is slender yet take note

I have beneath my petticoat
A comely body well designed
And a kallipygian behind
And it's no shame to say you'll find
My legs well-shaped and well-aligned
What's best of all I won't repeat
It is a mystery complete.

'I have good curves, I'm white of skin,
Not short and thick, or long and thin,
No sullen slut all girns and frowns,
No hanger for unironed gowns,
No óinseach either who, poor thing,
Catches fresh acne each spring.
Oh, you'd go far before you could
See a piece of young womanhood
More full of spirit and red blood.

'Were I like others that I know
Who dowdier and yet dowdier grow,
Ignorant, listless, and slow,
Too blind to mind that none regards,
Too dull, too shy, to play their cards;
Why then I'd have to give up hope,
Let go, and slither down the slope.

'But no one's ever seen me yet
In any place where men are met,
Or any spot where young and old
Ever a wake or funeral hold,
No match or race or dance there's been

Where throngs assemble on the green,
At which I've let myself be seen
Except well-dressed, from head to foot,
In clothes all chosen well to suit,
Just enough powder on my head,
On which a well-starched coif I spread,
And over that a hood of white
Graced with a set of ribbons bright.
The printed frock I wear I deck
With ruffs both at the wrist and neck
My scarlet cloak you'll rarely view
Without some aery facing new.
A faery queen might envy me
This linen apron which, you see,
Is covered with embroidery
Of plant and herb and bird and tree.
I've sharp stiletto heels with screws
To lift the insteps of my shoes.
Buckles, silk gloves and rings add grace
To hoops and bracelets and old lace.

    'No, don't think I've been backward, I
Am not unnaturally shy,
I've never kept myself from sight as
Would some poor trembling anchoritess.
I enter and I leave a place
With curtsies elegant with grace
And dignity of brown and face,
I'm fit to be seen anywhere,

I need not draw back when men stare.
I surely put myself on show,
To every hurling green I go,
To every bonfire, romp and gambol
To race and dance and match and ramble,
To every market-day and fair,
To Mass on Sunday I repair.
I go there to be seen by men,
If any are worth seeing then
They see me look, and look again.
In spite of all my bright attractions
And all my enterprising actions,
In spite of all my love, content
To offer much encouragement
They fooled and left me in the lurch,
Not one would go with me to church.
I spent my wits in that vain search.
Yet I've tried hard, and spent as well,
For fortunes such as tea-leaves tell
Or tinker wives with cards can spell,
A fortune – but it was a sell.

        'I tried all tricks, I played all tunes
By waxing or by waning moons
At Shrove and at All Hallow's tide.
At feasts such as our holy guide,
The Church, does through the year provide
My many games I vainly tried.
I'd pillow my head every night

Upon a fruit-packed stocking tight,
(Emblem of that fertility
Which seems, alas, not meant for me).
All Lent I fasted piously
And slimmed myself industriously
I dipped my slip against the stream
Yet did not of a husband dream
I swept beneath the cornstack too,
Hair, nailpairings in greeshugh threw,
The flail did on the hearth-stone lie,
My distaff in our limekiln I
Put; when the neighbours were not by,
I put my ball of yarn in theirs,
Yet nothing happens, no one cares.
Flax seed about our 'street' I spread,
And wrapped in straw a cabbage head
To be beneath mine in my bed.
Of every trick of which I tell
Some Devil's name would make a spell
Impregnant with the powers of hell ...

' ... Sure of the cure I've power to gain,
Seeking a philtre for my pain.
Liquors from dried-up herbs I wring
Which like myself, are withering.
Such druid spells shall surely bring
Some handsome lad or stripling free
At last to fall in love with me.

I've often seen it done e're this,
The recipes don't ever miss;
Sliced apples, powdered herbs have powers
To couple couples at all hours,
Magairlín meidhreach brings to view
What men and mandrakes have to do
And I'll be gladly gone into
As half of one or one of two.
Old druid aphrodisiacs
Thus make one beast that has two backs;
And other plants too I could name
Though some might think it ill became
My female modesty to mention
Either the means or the intention.
Leaves burnt with a mysterious smell
And other fearsome doings fell
I've used – but no, I must not tell.

'North Munster's wonder was aroused
To see one single spinster spoused.
She told me what she had to do,
I swore to keep it secret too,
So don't let on that I've told you:
From Shrove right on to Hallow's tide
When she at last was made a bride
She never ate a single bite
(Her yellow hair turned almost white)
And drank a gruesome kind of grog
(Such as would sicken any dog

81

Or turn the stomach of a hog,)
Brewed out of blowflies from the bog.
Long patience learns to look askance
On credit, give a cash advance
Of full and swift deliverance;
Or else, unless your visitation
Can cure my furious desperation
I'll find some desperate remedy
I'll strike and shall not spare, you'll see,
Even though it may go hard with me.'

7

Songs

Unfortunately, singing isn't restricted to poets. In Ireland it isn't restricted at all. Some of these ballads* are best enjoyed in their written form, but normally experienced pulled out of shape by somebody's drunken granny.

THE QUEEN OF LOVE

As I walked forth one evening fair down by a shady grove,
With hastening step I did draw near to where I spied my
    love,
As she lay sleeping on the grass, all with her beauty fair,
You might have sworn, had you seen that lass, that the
    Queen of Love lay there.

With loving arms I embraced about her slender waist,
First I kissed her ruby lips, and embraced her milk-white
    breast;

---

* From James N. Healy's *The Mercier Book of Irish Street Ballads.*

But when this fair maid she arose, all in a great surprise,
Her innocent looks stole away my heart by the rolling of
  her eyes.

She sighed, and cried, I am undone, thus Judas had
  betrayed.
If this be the way you have, kind sir, for to harm an innocent maid,
There's not a man in all this life would ruin a maid so
  young.
Her amiable speech stole away my heart by the moving
  of her tongue.

I love my love, and make no doubt but she loves me as
  well,
And if ever he frowns at my request, I will laugh at him
  as well;
While he proves constant I'll prove kind, and so we will
  agree,
And if ever I find he'll alter his mind, I will change as well
  as he.

There are twelve months in all the year, as I heard my
  mamma say,
Two of them I would choose to love, the months of June
  and May.
These are the months I choose to love, when the red
  roses spring,

And the other months I would choose to wed, when the
    small birds sweetly sing.

A young girl's love is hard to win, let them all say what
    they will,
For when you think you have them won, they're farther
    from you still.
Riches and honour are all they want, and all that they
    require,
While a pretty girl carries the keys of love, it is few she
    will admire.

THE DARK ARCHES

Along the dark arches I carelessly did stray,
There I met a dashing young spark that caus'd me delay,
'You've time enough,' said she, 'come let us have some
    chat,'
I thought she was an angel bright when I ogl'd her brown
    hat.

'Excuse me, miss,' said I, 'there is no time for to delay,
Moreover in those dark arches, I'd be liable to go astray;
Besides I'm not accustom'd to Dublin by any means.'
'Well,' said she, 'take me, and I'll escort you to the train.'

As we walked along together she talked of by-gone
    things,

The Russian Bear and Wellington and sweetly she could
    sing –
'Pop goes the weasel', 'Reef the Bed', and 'Boneys March',
She sang with such ability that echo'd ev'ry arch.

She took out an accordion and play'd many tunes,
'Come Warm Yourself' was the first, next, 'The Dashing
    Dragoon',
'Stem up the rock on Buterstown', 'nix-my-doly' and
    'Patrick's Day',
But the dark arches was the best of all that she could
    play.

The next she play'd was 'Ireland's Curse' and 'The
    Darling Jug of Punch',
Along with 'the Irish Jaunting Car', 'Garryown', and such
    –
The Russians they are falling fast tho holding it out
    brave
But Napoleon he keeps sure cards and that he'll take the
    knave.

Her lovely voice and notes they charmed myself so,
At length I got enchanted and from her I could not go,
She play'd up with such element, Apollo she'd delay,
Myself at once I quite forgot the coach and the railway.

You never heard of such value before in any age,

And if you too you'd say the same yourself I'll engage,
It's only three pence down to Dundrum besides there is
    no delay,
So hurra! for the dark arches, Dollymount and railway.

So you gents here get ready if for jaunting you're inclin'd,
You talk of Wilson's omnibus, but there is nothing like
    the line;
Oh, here she's coming up, return tickets and no delay,
Take care of the dark arches coming by the railway.

Now to conclude and finish I'm enraptured with
    Kingstown,
For why entroth I'll tell you there is beauty and renown
That evening sitting in my coach all along the railway,
I thought on the dark arches, the brown hat and dearest
    May.

CAN OF SPRING WATER

One evening in May as I carelessly strayed
Thro' Kingstown for sweet recreation,
I met with a lass on the way as I passed,
And gazed on she with great admiration,
Her features were grand and her action bland,
Her footstep the least did not falter,
She sung a fine song as she tripped all along,

And she going for a can of spring water.

I made bold, was sincere, the truth to declare
I requested the name of her parents,
While in the address much love I expressed,
In that I was ever so serious,
'Oh, kind sir,' said she, 'keep a distance from me,
Or you'll feel the revenge of my father,'
She says, 'no young man shall draw close to me
And I going for my can of spring water.'

'Then,' said I, 'dear maid don't of me be afraid,
At least I'll give you no reason,
And if you I'd meet on my way thro' the street,
Sure no one could deem it a treason,
And then if perhaps we strayed by the gaps,
And delayed a bit more than we oughter
Say 'tis by chance that we both met together
And you going for your can of spring water.'

'Now kind sir,' said she, 'I cannot agree,
I know you intend to disgrace me,
Your absence is better than your company,
Therefore now begone and don't tease me,
For if I consent and my time should be spent,
And you should forsake me hereafter,
I'd like to know then who'd draw close to me
And I going for my can of spring water.'

I said, 'My dear dame, the truth I'll explain,
Indeed I don't mean any harm,
But to forward the game if we done the same,
Sure that would create no alarm,
When nine months would be spent, We'd take flight
    as we meant
You would be blest with a son or a daughter,
You'd pray for the man who did draw near your can,
And you going for your can of spring water.'

'Without any joke I think you're a rogue,'
She says in a great fit of laughter,
'But indeed it is true I'll stray far with you,
But I am too much in dread of my father,
Because, then, the squire, as he would desire,
By far, you, my love, I would rather,
So give me your hand and draw near my can,
I'm going for my can of spring water.'

I gave her my hand and we put by her can,
I thought that we'd want to be talking,
It was down by a tower quite close to a river
Until we were there tired of walking,
But now that this maiden is married by chance
She can be cheerful and happy hereafter,
She will nimbly dance while baby will prance
And she going for her can of spring water.

8

A Country Man

Nobody better than a country man and his diary to acquaint us with the reality of Irish traditional love. Notice the livestock approach to women and the fact that much of the matchmaking information given in an earlier chapter is borne out here.

THE DIARY OF AN IRISH COUNTRYMAN
1827–1835*
HUMPHREY O'SULLIVAN

18 April 1827

... At midday gay sweet-voiced Maraed de Barra, myself and another person went to Desart Court along the same way I went on Easter Sunday. We walked through the dark evergreen pine woods where we were sheltered from the sun as we went along the fine winding paths which straightened out now and again. We could hear the lark's song in the nearby meadows, the shorter call of the blackbird, the thrush and all the smaller birds which

---

* From *The Diary of an Irish Countryman* – A Translation of *Cín Lae Amhlaoibh* by Tomás de Bhaldraithe.

seemed to be in harmony with Maraed de Barra's gentle, lively, melodious speech. We went astray in a dark shadowy little glen until we couldn't make out east from west or north from south. At long last, having gone through mossy hollows, clumps of brambles, slopes covered with ash trees, and evergreen pine groves, we reached Cluain Lachan with its ponds, pools, lakelets, streams and murmuring waterfalls. White ducks and spotted drakes were there, and the blackbirds were singing to each other in the bush-tops. 'I am tired,' said sweet, gentle, vivacious Maraed. 'So am I.' 'Let us sit down on the moss-covered rock.' 'Certainly.' Maraed dozed off to sleep with the murmuring of the waterfall. 'Croon wind, through the trees in the swamp. Don't blow noisily or threateningly!' The wind blew gently through the sleeping wanderer's hair and laid bare her neck as white as the swan on the lake. Her little lips were as red as the rowan and as sweet as honey. Her breasts like two snow-clad knolls rose and fell like the swell on the King's River. Her neat little buttocks and her pretty little legs were hidden by her satin dress, down to her small tidy feet. Two snipe flew off from a pool near us like arrows from a bow. My beautiful young lady started from her sound sleep. 'May there be no pool for you in Ireland ever again,' said I. 'May there not be.' 'The sun is setting. Let us be off home.' We went off, tired and weary, her arm in mine, her head on my shoulder, her eyes lowered to the ground. I never remember a more pleasant day.

12 July 1827

... Doctor Céitinn and I walked right across the bog, with Poll na Caillí west of us and Poll an Chapaill to the east, as far as Mocklers where we had a slice of baker's bread with butter and a strong drop of whiskey. We walked over the bog collecting wild plants: water-mint, bog-cotton, common self-heal (a small coarse plant with a purple head or flower), common milfoil, which has a thousand petals and a brown stalk.

We saw a lovely girl kneading wet turf. She had slender, firm feet, calves and knees as white as bog-cotton, rounded fair thighs which were bare almost to her plump buttocks. Her father was once a well-off farmer, but the difficulties of life caught up with him. He lost everything. The landlord took his crops. The tithe-collector took away the table, the pot and the bed with him, and they all drove him out to wander the roads, himself, his wife and his handsome young children. That is why he ended up in a small cabin at the foot of the mountain, and why his beautiful daughter was now kneading turf pulp.

27 December 1829

I continued on to Muileann an Bhró, a place where only a little snow had fallen during this week and the ice is thin. From this it can be concluded that the cold is more severe up in the mountains and in Gleann an Rí, along the King's River at Callan of the Ructions, than down near Waterford, where I got a hundred welcomes from Father Síomón Breatnach and his family. There was a fine meal ready for me. We had freshly salted loins of beef, white cabbage, roast goose with bread-stuffing, a leg of mutton and turnips, bacon and pullets, a roasted snipe. We had port and punch.

And there was something else there, Máire Bhreatnach, a fine, tall, rosy-cheeked, sandy-haired lady, with her well-shaped buttocks and full, firm, fair breasts. She is about thirty-five. Her skin is not very fine, as it has a slight trace of small-pox, but she is quiet and well-mannered, and has an honest gentle look. She would scarcely look at me, nor let me take her fair hand in mine, as she knows I came by invitation to court her. But the affair will come to nothing.

28 December 1829

I spent part of the day seeing Waterford City and the shipping there, and the rest of it courting fair Máire Bhreatnach. I think I managed to soften her heart, as she gave me to understand that she would come home with me. I told her many a pleasant story, as Fr Síomón Breatnach and the widow Murphy and her two nice young daughters stayed out of the way on purpose. We have only to wait till Twelfth Day to be married. I am getting a good dowry with her, and I think she will make a good stepmother for my four orphans, for she has an easy-going, friendly appearance, like her brother,

Síomón the priest ...

29 December 1829

... After breaking my fast, I moved homewards over the rough summits of the Walsh Mountains. A sharp north wind was blowing against me, and small snowflakes were falling hard and heavy on me.

She is a hard-earned woman, but a good thing is seldom got without paying for it.

SOURCES

Danaher, Kevin – *In Ireland Long Ago*, Mercier Cork, 1962.

Danaher, Kevin – *The Year in Ireland*, Mercier, Cork, 1972.

Healy, James N. – *The Mercier Book of Street Ballads, Volume One*, Mercier, Cork, 1967.

Kennelly, Brendan – *Love of Ireland: Poems from the Irish*, Mercier, Cork, 1989.

Merriman, Brian (translated by Cosslett Ó Cuinn) – *The Midnight Court*, Mercier, Cork, 1982.

Ó Catháin, Séamas – *The Bedside Book of Irish Folklore*, Mercier, Cork, 1980.

O'Farrell, Padraic – *Gems of Irish Wisdom: Irish Proverbs and Sayings*, Mercier, Cork, 1980.

O'Farrell, Padraic – *Superstitions of the Irish Country People*, Mercier, Cork, 1978.

O'Sullivan, Humphrey – *The Diary of an Irish Countryman* – A Translation of *Cín Lae Amhlaoibh* by Tomás de Bhaldraithe, Mercier 1979.

Power, Patrick C. – *The Book of Irish Curses*, Mercier, Cork, 1974.

Seehan, Sean – *Dictionary of Irish Quotations*, Mercier, Cork, 1993,

White, Carolyn – *A History of Irish Fairies*, Mercier, Cork, 1976.

Wilde, Lady (selected by M. Feehan) – *Quaint Irish Customs and Superstitions*, Mercier, Cork, 1988.

MORE MERCIER TITLES

THINGS IRISH

Anthony Bluett

Things Irish provides the reader with an entertaining and informative view of Ireland, seen through the practices, beliefs and everyday objects that seem to belong specifically to this country. Discarding the usual format of lengthy chapters on a variety of themes, the book uses short descriptive passages on anything from whiskey to standing stones, from May Day to hurling in order to create a distinctive image of Irish life. The reader is free to roam from topic to topic, from passage to passage, discovering a wealth of new and surprising facts and having a number of misguided beliefs put right.

FAVOURITE IRISH STORIES

Anthony Bluett

The publication of *Favourite Irish Stories* coincided with the fiftieth anniversary of the Mercier Press, founded in 1944. The stories selected are among the best published by Mercier Press over the last half century.

The stories range from undoubted classics of Irish literature like the work of Padraic Pearse and Daniel Corkery, to more recent favourites like John B. Keane and Brian Cleeve. It also includes stories from the oral tradition, with a selection from Eric Cross' celebrated and controversial *The Tailor and Ansty* and stories from Eamon Kelly, Ireland's best-loved seanchaí.